Diet recommendations for radiation- and chemotherapy

Please check these recommendations always with a nutrition consultant, therapist, doctor or dietician. The recipes and the list of ingredients are supporting the conventional medical therapy.
The calorie disclosures of fresh ingredients (fruit and vegetables) vary according to quality and time of harvest. The contents were checked by a dietician and a nutrition consultant for the Traditional Chinese Medicine (TCM).

Author:
©2017 Josef Miligui
www.ebns.at

Source:
The lists are created from the EBNS database for nutritional counseling. The database is used by dietitians, therapists and doctors for advising the patient / client.

Literature:
The specialist literature and the training documents of the German and Austrian dietary and traditional Chinese medicine serve as a knowledge base. We have used the documents as a basis of knowledge, adapted it to our experience and completed them.
http://di-book.com

Title Photo:
©2008 Erika Weixlbaumer

Production and publishing:
BoD – Books on Demand, Norderstedt
ISBN 9783746043944

Diet recommendations for DIETETICS - Changed nutrient requirements - Radiation- and chemotherapy

1 Treatment strategy 4
2 Avoid 4
3 Breakfast 4
4 Snack 5
5 Lunch 6
6 Afternoon 7
7 Dinner 7
8 Any time 8
9 Recipes 9
   9.1 Adzuki Bean and Rice Soup 9
   9.2 Apple - banana cream 9
   9.3 Apple sauce with raisins 10
   9.4 Barley mash with steamed pear 11
   9.5 Barley soup 11
   9.6 Basic recipe for a beef broth (clear) 12
   9.7 Basic recipe for a duck broth 13
   9.8 Basic recipe for a reissue soup (Congee) 13
   9.9 Basmati rice + Zucchini tofu dish 14
   9.10 Bath with lavender 15
   9.11 Bitter lemon drink 15
   9.12 Breakfast - Rice with fruits 15
   9.13 Cold cherry soup with curd cheese dumpling 16
   9.14 Compote from apples 17
   9.15 Compote of local fruit and dried fruit 17
   9.16 Corn coffee with cardamom 18
   9.17 Creamy potatoes with cauliflower 18
   9.18 Curry rice with raisins and nuts 19
   9.19 Figs with mozzarella and honey 20
   9.20 Fresh full-grain porridge 21
   9.21 Fried apple 21
   9.22 Fruit juice 22
   9.23 Grated apple 22
   9.24 Hearty polenta mash 23
   9.25 Honey milk 23
   9.26 Lentils and rice stew 24
   9.27 Mango banana yoghurt drink ice cold 24
   9.28 Millet with pears 25
   9.29 Miso soup with tofu 26

9.30	Oat Congee	26
9.31	Oat flakes with aromatic spices	27
9.32	Oyster mushrooms with asparagus	27
9.33	Plum Cake	28
9.34	Porridge	29
9.35	Porridge with cherries	29
9.36	Quick flakes with compote or jam	30
9.37	Rhubarb and apple jelly	31
9.38	Ribbon noodles with leaf spinach	31
9.39	Rice congee with chicken liver and buckthorn fruit	32
9.40	Rice congee with honey pear and black sesame	33
9.41	Rice with parsnips	33
9.42	Roasted millet with Celery sticks	34
9.43	Roasted nuts	35
9.44	Rosemary Potatoes	35
9.45	Semolina porridge with banana	36
9.46	Soup with egg yolk	36
9.47	Spelled with fruit and nuts	37
9.48	Supplementary nutrition	37
9.49	Sweet rice with apples	38
9.50	Sweet-savory barley salad	39
9.51	Tea Black tea (Russian tea)	39
9.52	Tea from juniper berry	40
9.53	Tea Green tea	41
9.54	Tomato with mozzarella	41
9.55	Vanilla cream with berries	42
9.56	Vanilla pudding	42
9.57	Whole milk cereal mash	43
9.58	Yogurt with honey and nuts	43
10	Effects of food	44
10.1	Use ingredients: recommendable	44
10.2	Use ingredients: yes	44
10.3	Use ingredients: little	51
10.4	Do not use contra-acting foods	51
11	Herbs and their effects	52
11.1	Basil (fresh)	52
11.2	Coriander	52
11.3	Herbs various	52
11.4	Cress	52
11.5	Lavender blossoms	52
11.6	Lovage	52
11.7	Oregano dried	52
11.8	Parsley	52

11.9	Peppermint	53
11.10	Rosemary	53
11.11	Sage	53
11.12	Black caraway	53
11.13	Thyme dried	53
11.14	Lemon Balm (fresh)	53
12 Basics of Nutrition		54
12.1	Nutrition	54
12.2	Recipes	56
12.3	Foodstuffs	56
12.4	Herbs	57
13 Other dietic-books		58

1 Treatment strategy

In radiotherapy, care must be taken to ensure adequate energy and nutrient supply, whereby the individual symptoms must be considered in the dietary therapy. A further main note is the often occurring lack of nutrition. A healthy, balanced mixed food is to provide all the necessary nutrients as well as vitamins and minerals, paying particular attention to the adequate protein supply.

If organs of the digestive system or areas of the mouth are inflamed, special attention should be paid to other special diet.

2 Avoid

High-dose antioxidants in the form of food supplements can adversely affect the effects of radiation therapy, but the antioxidant content in fruits and vegetables when required for consumption is considered harmless.

3 Breakfast

	kkal. per serving
Adzuki Bean and Rice Soup	199
Apple - banana cream	110
Apple sauce with raisins	73
Barley mash with steamed pear	113
Barley soup	265
Breakfast - Rice with fruits	230
Compote from apples	67

Compote of local fruit and dried fruit 45
Corn coffee with cardamom 3
Creamy potatoes with cauliflower 332
Curry rice with raisins and nuts 275
Fried apple 408
Fruit juice 175
Grated apple 120
Hearty polenta mash 262
Mango banana yoghurt drink ice cold 121
Millet with pears 213
Miso soup with tofu 51
Oat Congee 162
Oat flakes with aromatic spices 280
Oyster mushrooms with asparagus 316
Plum Cake 502
Porridge 207
Porridge with cherries 227
Quick flakes with compote or jam 189
Rhubarb and apple jelly 180
Ribbon noodles with leaf spinach 722
Rice congee with honey pear and black sesame 158
Rice with parsnips 206
Roasted millet with Celery sticks 400
Roasted nuts 973
Rosemary Potatoes 188
Semolina porridge with banana 307
Soup with egg yolk 173
Spelled with fruit and nuts 289
Sweet rice with apples 155
Sweet-savory barley salad 511
Tea Black tea (Russian tea) 7
Tea from juniper berry 10
Tea Green tea 2
Vanilla cream with berries 278
Vanilla pudding 254
Whole milk cereal mash 205
Yogurt with honey and nuts 258

4   Snack

Adzuki Bean and Rice Soup 199
Apple - banana cream 110
Apple sauce with raisins 73

Creamy potatoes with cauliflower 332
Figs with mozzarella and honey 415
Plum Cake 502

5 Lunch

Adzuki Bean and Rice Soup 199
Apple sauce with raisins 73
Barley mash with steamed pear 113
Barley soup 265
Basmati rice + Zucchini tofu dish 145
Cold cherry soup with curd cheese dumpling 320
Compote from apples 67
Compote of local fruit and dried fruit 45
Corn coffee with cardamom 3
Creamy potatoes with cauliflower 332
Curry rice with raisins and nuts 275
Fried apple 408
Fruit juice 175
Grated apple 120
Hearty polenta mash 262
Lentils and rice stew 232
Mango banana yoghurt drink ice cold 121
Millet with pears 213
Miso soup with tofu 51
Oat Congee 162
Oyster mushrooms with asparagus 316
Porridge 207
Porridge with cherries 227
Rhubarb and apple jelly 180
Ribbon noodles with leaf spinach 722
Rice congee with chicken liver and buckthorn fruit 175
Rice congee with honey pear and black sesame 158
Rice with parsnips 206
Roasted millet with Celery sticks 400
Roasted nuts 973
Rosemary Potatoes 188
Semolina porridge with banana 307
Soup with egg yolk 173
Supplementary nutrition 1045
Sweet rice with apples 155
Sweet-savory barley salad 511
Tea Black tea (Russian tea) 7

Tea from juniper berry 10
Tea Green tea... 2
Tomato with mozzarella 436
Whole milk cereal mash 205
Yogurt with honey and nuts... 258

6 Afternoon

Apple - banana cream.. 110
Apple sauce with raisins.. 73
Creamy potatoes with cauliflower 332
Figs with mozzarella and honey 415
Plum Cake 502
Vanilla pudding 254

7 Dinner

Adzuki Bean and Rice Soup... 199
Apple sauce with raisins.. 73
Barley soup... 265
Basmati rice + Zucchini tofu dish.. 145
Cold cherry soup with curd cheese dumpling............................. 320
Compote from apples.. 67
Compote of local fruit and dried fruit... 45
Corn coffee with cardamom.. 3
Creamy potatoes with cauliflower 332
Curry rice with raisins and nuts... 275
Fresh full-grain porridge 336
Fried apple.. 408
Fruit juice... 175
Grated apple... 120
Hearty polenta mash... 262
Honey milk... 88
Lentils and rice stew... 232
Mango banana yoghurt drink ice cold 121
Millet with pears 213
Miso soup with tofu 51
Oat Congee 162
Porridge.. 207
Porridge with cherries 227
Ribbon noodles with leaf spinach 722
Rice congee with chicken liver and buckthorn fruit...................... 175
Rice congee with honey pear and black sesame 158
Rice with parsnips.. 206

Roasted millet with Celery sticks 400
Roasted nuts.. 973
Rosemary Potatoes... 188
Semolina porridge with banana 307
Sweet rice with apples.. 155
Sweet-savory barley salad 511
Tea Black tea (Russian tea) 7
Tea from juniper berry... 10
Tea Green tea.. 2
Tomato with mozzarella 436
Whole milk cereal mash 205

8   Any time

Apple sauce with raisins - Also for babies from 6th month 73
Basic recipe for a reissue soup (Congee) 140
Compote from apples.. 67
Compote of local fruit and dried fruit.. 45
Corn coffee with cardamom... 3
Creamy potatoes with cauliflower 332
Fruit juice.. 175
Grated apple.. 120
Mango banana yoghurt drink ice cold 121
Miso soup with tofu 51
Oat Congee 162
Porridge with cherries 227
Rice congee with honey pear and black sesame 158
Rice with parsnips.. 206
Roasted nuts.. 973
Semolina porridge with banana 307
Tea Black tea (Russian tea) 7
Tea from juniper berry... 10
Tea Green tea.. 2
Whole milk cereal mash 205
Yogurt with honey and nuts... 258

9 Recipes

(recommendable) = You can use more.
(little) = You should use less than specified or omit.

9.1 Adzuki Bean and Rice Soup

Strengthens spleen, heart, kidney and stomach, supports urination, improves blood circulation, reduces inflammation.
Cooking time approx. 2 hours
Calories p. portion: 199
1 portions
Allergens:

Quantity of ingredients
Adzuki beans 8 table spoons / 40g. (yes)
Rice round grain 2 table spoons / 20g. (yes)
Water 1 1/2 cups / 200g. (yes)
Honey 1 table spoon / 8g. (recommended)

Cooking instructions:
Boil soaked adzuki beans and round grain rice in a ratio of 4: 1 in water until a thin pulp has formed. Sweet as needed; possibly puree.

Effect: This recipe strengthens kidney, spleen and stomach and is particularly suitable for mothers with too little milk flow.

9.2 Apple - banana cream

Regulates gastrointestinal function, provides vitamin C, cholesterol lowering, reduces inflammation, diuretic, improves blood circulation.
Cooking time approx. 15 min
Calories p. portion: 110
4 portions
Allergens:

Quantity of ingredients
Apple (sour) 7/8 lbs / 400g. (recommended)
Water 3/4 cup - 6 oz / 200g. (yes)
Orange peel 1/4 piece / 5g. (yes)

Lemon peel 1/2 piece / 2g. (yes)
Sugar brown 2 teaspoons / 6g. (recommended)
Cinnamon sticks 1 piece / 0g. (yes)
Banana 1 piece / 150g. (yes)
Acerola fruit nectar or powder 1 teaspoon / 2g. (yes)
Orange juice 1/2 piece / 50g. (recommended)
Lemon juice 1 table spoon / 10g. (yes)

Cooking instructions:
Cut the apple into fine slices, bring water to boil and add the apple slices, orange- and lemon peel, sugar and cinnamon and simmer about 7 minutes. The apples should be almost soft. Remove acerola and the cinnamon stick.
Mix the apple, the banana, the orange juice and the lemon juice.

9.3 Apple sauce with raisins

Stops diarrhea, promotes digestion, appetizing, relieves diarrhea, activates carbohydrate metabolism.
Cooking time approx. 25 min
Calories p. portion: 74
10 portions
Allergens: O

Quantity of ingredients
Apple (sweet) 2,2 lbs / 1000g. (recommended)
Water 1/2 cup / 100g. (yes)
Raisins 1/8 lbs - 2oz / 50g. (yes)

Cooking instructions:
Wash, peel and quarter the apples and remove the core. Put the apples with the water in a pot. Wash the raisins with hot water and add them. Cook at low heat for about 10 minutes, then allow to cool. For children up to 10 months, mash in the blender finely. For the larger ones, crush with the potato steamer. Fill and seal in a freezer or empty yoghurt jug. Close the yoghurt jug. Freeze in the shock freezer.
If necessary, thaw at room temperature for about 6 hours. (Lasting about 4 months).
The fruit mousse is intended as dessert or intermediate meal. It has an anti-digestive effect. In case of diarrhea give better banana.

9.4 Barley mash with steamed pear

Promotes digestion, supports urination, promotes spleen, diuretic, forcing spleen, relaxes, promotes perspiration.
Cooking time approx. 25 min
Calories p. portion: 114
5 portions
Allergens: A

Quantity of ingredients
Water 10 cups / 1200g. (yes)
Barley 1 cup / 120g. (yes)
Ginger fresh 2 slices / 2g. (yes)
Cardamom 3 capsules / 1g. (yes)
Salt 1 pinch / 1g. (little)
Pear 1 piece / 200g. (yes)
Sugar cane sugar 1/2 teaspoon / 5g. (recommended)

Cooking instructions:
Grind coarse the barley and roast it dry. Add hot water, add ginger and cardamom and let it swell to a pulp in low heat. Peel and dice the pear and boil for 10 minutes with a little water. At the end, add the stewed pear, a little butter and sweetener.

Variant: If you want to go fast, you can use barley flakes instead of shot.

9.5 Barley soup

Diuretic, forcing spleen, supports urination, stimulates liver function, antioxidativ, promotes digestion, detoxifying, reduces blood lipids, stimulates, dissolves stagnation.
Cooking time approx. 25 min
Calories p. portion: 265
2 portions
Allergens: A

Quantity of ingredients
Barley 1 cup / 120g. (yes)
Salt 1 pinch / 1g. (little)
Ginger fresh 1/2 teaspoon / 1g. (yes)
Olive oil 1 table spoon / 10g. (yes)
Parsley 2 table spoons / 30g. (yes)
Water 1 1/2 cups / 240g. (yes)

Cooking instructions:
Roast the barley in the pan, then grind it to the ground, and boil with water, some salt and ginger to a mash. Before serving add oil and parsley.

Variant: You can add a better taste to the dish if you cook it with prepared vegetable or meat broth.

9.6 Basic recipe for a beef broth (clear)

Strengthens muscles, tendons and bones, reduces blood pressure, strengthens immune system, prevents cancer, reduces radiation damage, stimulates digestion, reduces pain, promotes digestion, diuretic. Rosemary stimulates digestion.
Cooking time approx. 4-8 hours
Calories p. portion: 114
10 portions
Allergens: O

Quantity of ingredients
Beef soup meat 1,1 lbs / 500g. (yes)
Beef meatbones 5/8 oz / 200g. (yes)
Vinegar (Red wine vinegar) 1 dash / 3g. (yes)
Juniper berry 8 pieces / 6g. (yes)
Rosemary 1 pinch / 1g. (yes)
Carrot 3 pieces / 210g. (yes)
Parsnip 2 pieces / 300g. (yes)
Leek 1 piece / 200g. (yes)
Ginger fresh 1/2 teaspoon / 5g. (yes)
Lovage 1 stem / 15g. (yes)
Clove 2 pieces / 2g. (yes)
Pimento 6 pieces / 12g. (yes)
Anise (Common Fennel) 2 pieces / 1g. (yes)
Salt 1 teaspoon / 5g. (little)
Water 3,3 lbs / 1300g. (yes)

Cooking instructions:
Heat water, a dash of red wine vinegar, some juniper berries, a little rosemary, bones and meat till it boils; add carrot, parsnip, leek, ginger, lovage, clove, allspice, star anise and a little salt; simmer for 4-8 hours then strain.
Refrigerate for later use.

9.7 Basic recipe for a duck broth

Forcing spleen, strengthens blood, supports urination, reduces blood pressure, strengthens immune system, prevents cancer, reduces radiation damage.
Cooking time approx. 2-3 hours
Calories p. portion: 61
6 portions
Allergens: L

Quantity of ingredients
Duck (heart) 5/8 oz / 200g. (yes)
Water 2 cup / 450g. (yes)
Duck (slaughtered) 1/4 lbs - 4oz / 100g. (yes)
Carrot 2 pieces / 100g. (yes)
Celery root 1/2 piece / 600g. (yes)

Cooking instructions:
Cook duck pieces with vegetables for 2-3 hours. Sift broth through a fine sieve and refrigerate for later use.

The innards can be reused: You cut them finely and leaves them for a few minutes with fresh vegetables in the broth draw. Sprinkle with parsley before serving.

9.8 Basic recipe for a reissue soup (Congee)

Low fat content, for the drainage of the body overweight and high blood pressure.
Cooking time approx. 2-4 hours
Calories p. portion: 140
3 portions
Allergens:

Quantity of ingredients
Rice variety any 1 cup / 120g. (yes)
Water 6 cups / 700g. (yes)

Cooking instructions:
Cook rice and water in a ratio of about 1: 6. The amount of water determines the thickness of the mash (matter of taste).
Put the rice in a saucepan with a heavy lid. It is important to simmer the rice after a short boil on the slightest flame, otherwise it burns.
Boil the rice for 2-4 hours. The longer he cooks, the more he

strengthens.

If you want to eat the dish for breakfast, you can put the rice on just before bedtime.

To be on the safe side, you should first check the behavior of your pot and cooker under observation for a similar amount of time, so that nothing burns.

Refrigerate for later use.

9.9   Basmati rice + Zucchini tofu dish

Diuretic, supports urination, harmonizes spleen and stomach, reduces flatulence, good to fight body overweight and high blood pressure. Antioxidativ, promotes digestion, perspiration, reduces blood lipids, forcing spleen.

Cooking time approx. 20 min
Calories p. portion: 146
4 portions
Allergens: E

Quantity of ingredients
Soy Tofu 5/8 lbs - 8oz / 250g. (yes)
Olive oil 2 table spoons / 6g. (yes)
Coriander 1/2 teaspoon / 4g. (yes)
Ginger fresh 1/2 teaspoon / 4g. (yes)
Rice Basmati 1/2 cup / 60g. (yes)
Water 3 cups / 200g. (yes)
Zucchini 1 piece / 700g. (yes)

Cooking instructions:
Cut tofu cubes and marinate with olive oil, tamari, crushed coriander and ginger. Leave at least 1 hour.

Cook Basmati rice with the water. You can season with onion and cardamom.

Roast zucchini and tofu in pan in the hot oil for approx. 5-7 min.

Serve rice and tofu on a plate.

Add the parsley.

Can also be used as a salad for the home and on the go.

9.10 Bath with lavender

Calming, regenerates the central nervous system. Good to fight sleep disorders, loss of appetite and nervous intestinal complaints.
Cooking time approx. 10 min
Calories p. portion: 0
2 portions
Allergens:

Quantity of ingredients
Lavender blossoms 1 sachet / 5g. (yes)

Instructions:
Put a tied bag with the lavender in the water and let it soak for 10 minutes. The bag can be squeezed several times before removing it.

9.11 Bitter lemon drink

Appetizing
Cooking time approx. 5 min
Calories p. portion: 130
1 portions
Allergens:

Quantity of ingredients
Bitter Lemon 1 cup / 250g. (recommended)

9.12 Breakfast - Rice with fruits

Good to fight blood circulation disorders, thrombose, risk of embolism, high blood pressure, a headache, heart attack and stroke. Encourages blood build-up, promotes digestion, reduces Inflammation.
Cooking time approx. 10 min - 3 hours
Calories p. portion: 231
3 portions
Allergens: GHO

Quantity of ingredients

Basic recipe for a rice soup (Congee) 6 cups / 500g. (yes)
Cow's milk (whole milk 3.5% fat) 1/2 to 1 cup / 80g. (recommended)
Honey 1 table spoon / 10g. (recommended)
Butter organic 1 table spoon / 15g. (yes)
Dates dried 1 table spoon / 15g. (yes)
Fig 1 table spoon / 15g. (yes)
Apple (sour) 1 piece / 200g. (recommended)
Hazelnuts 1/2 teaspoon / 5g. (yes)
Almond 1/2 teaspoon / 5g. (yes)
Cinnamon ground 1 pinch / 1g. (yes)

Cooking instructions:

Cook rice congee according to basic recipe or use pre-cooked.
Make it with the milk more fluid and sweet with honey.
Fry the fruits and nuts in butter and mix with the finished rice soup, add chopped dates, figs and the apple.

9.13 Cold cherry soup with curd cheese dumpling

Improves blood circulation, reduces inflammation, good to fight weakness, belching, diabetes, acute or chronic obstruction of the bowel.
Laxative, stimulates digestion, cleans the intestinal flora.
Cooking time approx. 2 hours and more
Calories p. portion: 320
2 portions
Allergens: GO

Quantity of ingredients

Cherry compote 7/8 lbs / 450g. (recommended)
Agar agar (kelp) 1/2 teaspoon / 1,5g. (yes)
Curd cheese 20% 1/4 lbs - 4oz / 100g. (yes)
Sour cream 15% fat 1/8 lbs - 2oz / 50g. (recommended)
Vanilla sugar natural 1 package / 1g. (yes)
Sugar brown 1 table spoon / 10g. (recommended)
Cinnamon ground 1 pinch / 0,5g. (yes)
Lemon peel 1 pinch / 1g. (yes)

Cooking instructions:

Strain the cherry compote.
Finely puree half of the cherries with the cherry juice using a blender and pass through a sieve.
Stir agar agar powder with cold water until smooth.

Bring the cherry puree to boil while stirring.
Mix in the agar-agar and cook the cherry puree for 1 minute while stirring.
Spread hot cherry puree on two soup plates.
Sprinkle the remaining cherries into the soup.
Cool down cherry soup for 2 hours until lightly gelled.
Use the hand mixer to stir the cord cheese, sour cream, sugar, vanilla sugar, cinnamon and lemon zest into a smooth, firm cream.
From the cream with the tablespoon, prick small dumplings and put them into the cherry soup.

9.14 Compote from apples

Apple (sweet) stops diarrhea, promotes digestion, appetizing, harmonizes the stomach. Warms stomach and spleen, improves blood circulation.
Cooking time approx. 10 min
Calories p. portion: 67
2 portions
Allergens:

Quantity of ingredients
Apple (sweet) 1 piece / 220g. (recommended)
Water 1 1/2 cups / 220g. (yes)
Cinnamon ground 1 pinch / 1g. (yes)

Cooking instructions:
Cook the apples (organic) with the skin and seeds. Sprinkle with cinnamon.

9.15 Compote of local fruit and dried fruit

Promotes digestion, supports urination, stops diarrhea, promotes digestion, appetizing, relieves diarrhea. Warms stomach and spleen, improves blood circulation.
Cooking time approx. 15 min
Calories p. portion: 45
4 portions
Allergens:

Quantity of ingredients
Apple (sweet) 1 piece / 150g. (recommended)
Pear 1 piece / 150g. (yes)
Cinnamon ground 1 pinch / 0,2g. (yes)
Lemon peel 1/2 teaspoon / 2g. (yes)
Water 2 cup / 500g. (yes)

Cooking instructions:
Cook the apple and pear with the dried fruit until soft. Sprinkle with cinnamon and lemon zest (organic).

9.16 Corn coffee with cardamom

Diuretic, forcing spleen, supports urination, relaxes, reduces fat.
Cooking time approx. 5 min
Calories p. portion: 3
1 portions
Allergens:

Quantity of ingredients
Cereal coffee 1 table spoon / 15g. (yes)
Cardamom 2 cores / 1g. (yes)
Water 1 cup / 120g. (yes)

Cooking instructions:
Boil water, coffee, sugar and cardamom. Let it set for one min before drinking.

9.17 Creamy potatoes with cauliflower

Improves digestion, regenerates skin, supports urination, lowers cholesterol, stimulates liver function, detoxifying.
Cooking time approx. 30 min
Calories p. portion: 332
1 portions
Allergens: CG

Quantity of ingredients
Potato 3/8 lbs - 6oz / 150g. (yes)
Cauliflower 1/8 lbs - 2oz / 50g. (yes)
Cow's milk (whole milk 3.5% fat) 2 table spoons / 30g. (recommended)
Cream, sweet 30% 1 table spoon / 10g. (recommended)
Butter organic 1 teaspoon / 10g. (yes)
Parsley 1 teaspoon / 3g. (yes)
Chicken yolk 1 piece / 25g. (yes)

Cooking instructions:
Wash the potatoes under running water, thoroughly wash the cauliflower in stagnant water.
Divide the cauliflower florets into small buds, cut the stems into pieces about 1 cm in size.
Peel the potatoes and cut into 2 cm cubes.
Heat the milk with the cream in a saucepan, add the potatoes and the cauliflower. Cook on low heat for about 15 minutes.
Put the vegetables in a plate, add the butter, the chopped parsley and the egg yolk and lightly knead and mix everything with a fork.

9.18 Curry rice with raisins and nuts

Stops diarrhea, promotes digestion, appetizing, harmonizes the stomach, improves blood circulation, improves medication effect, stimulates appetite, increases body temperature, promotes perspiration.
Cooking time approx. 30 min
Calories p. portion: 275
4 portions
Allergens: HO

Quantity of ingredients
Sunflower oil 1 table spoon / 15g. (yes)
Onion white 1 piece / 50g. (yes)
Curry 1/2 teaspoon / 2g. (yes)
Rice wild (nature rice) 1 cup / 120g. (yes)
Salt 1 pinch / 1g. (little)
White wine 1/2 cup / 125g. (little)
Lemon Alternatively for white wine / g. (yes)
Peppers powder 1 pinch / 1g. (yes)
Apple (sweet) 2 pieces / 300g. (recommended)
Raisins 2 table spoons / 25g. (yes)
Walnuts 2 table spoons / 25g. (recommended)
Water 6 cups / 500g. (yes)

Cooking instructions:
Heat oil in a pot; fry chopped onions until glassy; add the curry and let it foam for a short time; then fry the raw rice for a few minutes over a gentle heat, stirring constantly; Salt, a dash of white wine or lemon juice, rose paprika, sweet apples chopped, raisins, chopped, roasted nuts added; pour hot water on it until well covered; simmer until the rice is cooked.

Goes well with: carrot and fennel vegetables, legumes with boiled vegetables, sliced poultry with ginger and mushrooms.

9.19 Figs with mozzarella and honey

Promotes digestion, reduces inflammation, bloating and nausea, relaxing and reassuring, relieves pain, detoxifying, blood stilling, forcing spleen and digestive system, detoxifying, bactericide.
Cooking time approx. 10 min
Calories p. portion: 415
1 portions
Allergens: GO

Quantity of ingredients
Fig 4 pieces / 100g. (yes)
Mozzarella 1 piece / 50g. (yes)
Basil (fresh) 1/2 bunch / 50g. (yes)
Honey 2 table spoons / 24g. (recommended)
Pepper (ground) 1 pinch / 0,1g. (yes)
Grapeseed oil 1 table spoon / 12g. (yes)
Vinegar Aceto Balsamico white 1 table spoon / 12g. (yes)

Cooking instructions:
Quarter fresh figs, dice buffalo mozzarella, pluck basil leaves.
Mix a dressing with light balsamic vinegar, grapeseed oil and honey and season to taste.
Place the figs on the edge of the appropriate plate. Spread the mozzarella cubes and season with black pepper.
Spread whole or roughly sliced basil leaves over it and moisten with the marinade.
Spiced pizza bread goes perfectly with it.

9.20 Fresh full-grain porridge

Regulates gastrointestinal function. Reduces Inflammation, relieves pain, detoxifying, bactericide.
Cooking time approx. 15 min
Calories p. portion: 336
1 portions
Allergens: AG

Quantity of ingredients
Spelled wholemeal flour 1 oz / 25g. (yes)
Cow's milk (whole milk 3.5% fat) 3/4 cup - 6 oz / 200g. (recommended)
Honey 1 teaspoon / 3g. (recommended)
Banana 1 piece / 120g. (yes)

Cooking instructions:
Grind the cereal grains into a flour mill. You may also be able to use a coffee grinder, but then grind twice. Stir the flour with the milk in a saucepan and bring it to boil over medium heat. Cook the porridge on low heat for 4-5 minutes while stirring. Then add the honey. Crush the banana with a fork and pull it under the porridge.

9.21 Fried apple

Good to fight acute or chronic constipation of the intestine, warming stomach and spleen, improves blood circulation. Good to fight kidney weakness, back pain and abdominal pain, impotence.
Cooking time approx. 30 min
Calories p. portion: 408
4 portions
Allergens: GH

Quantity of ingredients
Apple (sour) 4 pieces / 500g. (recommended)
Hazelnuts 1/8 lbs - 2oz / 50g. (yes)
Almond 1/8 lbs - 2oz / 50g. (yes)
Cinnamon ground 1 pinch / 0,2g. (yes)
Vanilla sugar natural 1 package / 3g. (yes)
Cow's milk (whole milk 3.5% fat) 2 table spoons / 24g. (recommended)
Sugar - icing sugar 2 table spoons / 36g. (recommended)
Cinnamon ground 1 pinch / 1g. (yes)
Yoghurt vanilla 3 cups / 750g. (yes)

Cooking instructions:
Wash the apples, cut off a lid, cut out the core casing with a teaspoon so that the apple remains a tight bottom.
Mix nuts, almonds, fructose, milk, vanilla sugar, cinnamon well. Fill into the apples. Put the covers back on.
Bake in preheated oven at 180 ° C for approx. 20 minutes.
Mix icing sugar and cinnamon.
Spread vanilla yoghurt on plate, place 1 baked apple on each, sprinkle with cinnamon-powdered sugar mixture.
Serve hot immediately!

9.22 Fruit juice

Stops diarrhea, promotes digestion, appetizing, harmonizes the stomach, relieves pain, detoxifying, reduces blood pressure, strengthens immune system, prevents cancer, reduces radiation damage.
Cooking time approx. 10 min
Calories p. portion: 176
2 portions
Allergens:

Quantity of ingredients
Orange 2 pieces / 150g. (yes)
Apple (sweet) 4 pieces / 300g. (recommended)
Carrot 2 pieces / 150g. (yes)
Honey 1 table spoon / 10g. (recommended)

Cooking instructions:
Peel oranges and carrots. Cut all ingredients into cubes so that they fit into the juicer and juice. Sweet with honey.

9.23 Grated apple

Eat 3 times a day - Apple (sour) scraped and brown is stuffing. Relieves diarrhea.
Cooking time approx. 10 min
Calories p. portion: 120
1 portions
Allergens:

Quantity of ingredients
Apple (sour) 1 piece / 200g. (recommended)

Cooking instructions:
Peel apple and grate as fine as possible. Leave for at least 5 minutes until it turns brown.

9.24 Hearty polenta mash

Strengths spleen and stomach, promotes watering, promotes digestion, detoxifying, promotes perspiration, reduces blood lipids, stimulates, dissolves stagnation, stimulates appetite, dissolves stagnation.
Cooking time approx. 10 min
Calories p. portion: 262
2 portions
Allergens:

Quantity of ingredients
Corn Grease (Polenta) 1 cup / 120g. (yes)
Onion (spring onion) 2 pieces / 40g. (yes)
Ginger fresh 1/2 teaspoon / 2g. (yes)
Nutmeg 1 pinch / 1g. (yes)
Salt 1 pinch / 1g. (little)
Olive oil 1 table spoon / 10g. (yes)
Turmeric (yellow root) 1 pinch / 1g. (yes)
Water 1 1/2 cups / 240g. (yes)

Cooking instructions:
Stir in the polenta in boiling water and let it swell for 7 min. Add green onion, grated ginger, turmeric, nutmeg, salt and olive oil and wait for 3 more minutes.

9.25 Honey milk

Calming, good to fight insomnia. Little laxative. Relieves pain, detoxifying, bactericide.
Cooking time approx. 5 min
Calories p. portion: 88
1 portions
Allergens: G

Quantity of ingredients
Cow's milk (whole milk 3.5% fat) 1 cup / 120g. (recommended)
Honey 1 teaspoon / 4g. (recommended)

Cooking instructions:
Heat the milk gently and add the honey. Drink in small sips.

9.26 Lentils and rice stew

Promotes spleen and kidney, is very nutritious, reduces blood pressure, strengthens immune system. Good to fight blood circulation disorders, thromboses, risk of embolism, high blood pressure, a headache. Strengthens heart and kidney, diuretic, calms the stomach, promotes digestion.
Cooking time approx. 25 min
Calories p. portion: 232
3 portions
Allergens: LNO

Quantity of ingredients
Lentils 1/4 lbs - 4oz / 100g. (yes)
Water 5 cups / 500g. (yes)
Rice variety any 1 cup / 120g. (yes)
Sesame oil 1 table spoon / 10g. (yes)
Carrot 2 pieces / 150g. (yes)
Celery sticks 2 rods / 20g. (yes)
Cumin (Caraway seed) 1 pinch / 0,2g. (yes)
Salt 1 pinch / 0,5g. (little)
Vinegar (Apple vinegar) 1 dash / 2g. (yes)
Parsley 2 table spoons / 18g. (yes)

Cooking instructions:
Soak the dry lentils the day before.
Heat sesame oil in a hot pot; cut carrot and celery into small pieces and sauté; add rice, a pinch of cumin and lentils and heat till it boils.
If the lenses are soft, add salt; season with a little vinegar and garnish with parsley.

Variant: In summer you can omit the cumin and add fresh green peas, Chinese cabbage or celery.

9.27 Mango banana yoghurt drink ice cold

Good to fight loss of appetite, oral mucosa inflammation. Regulates gastrointestinal function, chronic constipation. Prevents cancer. Diuretic, forcing spleen.

Cooking time approx. 5 min
Calories p. portion: 121
2 portions
Allergens: G

Quantity of ingredients
Mango juice 1/2 cup / 100g. (recommended)
Yogurt (natural, 1.5% fat) 1/4 lbs - 4oz / 100g. (yes)
Mineral water 1/2 cup / 100g. (yes)
Banana 1/2 piece / 150g. (yes)
Acerola fruit nectar or powder 1 teaspoon / 2g. (yes)

Cooking instructions:
Mix all the ingredients and 2-3 ice cubes in a blender.

9.28 Millet with pears

Refreshing and nourishing, promotes digestion, supports urination, good to fight cough, promotes perspiration, reduces blood lipids, stimulates, dissolves stagnation, forces liver, strengthens the muscles, lowers cholesterol, antiparasitic.
Cooking time approx. 35 min
Calories p. portion: 213
5 portions
Allergens: G

Quantity of ingredients
Millet 1 cup / 120g. (yes)
Water 1 1/2 cups / 200g. (yes)
Grape juice red 1 1/2 cups / 240g. (recommended)
Pear 4 pieces / 600g. (yes)
Ginger fresh 1/2 teaspoon / 2g. (yes)
Salt 1 pinch / 1g. (little)
Acerola fruit nectar or powder 1 teaspoon / 2g. (yes)
Cocoa 1 pinch / 1g. (yes)
Sunflower seeds 2 table spoons / 4g. (yes)
Barley malt 1/2 teaspoon / 2g. (yes)
Cream, sweet 30% 2 teaspoons / 20g. (recommended)

Cooking instructions:
Simmer the millet for 5 min and let it swell for another 30 min.

Then: In a hot pot, heat some grape juice; add chopped pears, very little grated ginger, a pinch of salt, acerola, a pinch of cocoa and sauté briefly; add the boiled millet, sunflower seeds, some barley malt to taste, 1 tsp cream per serving or a little butter.

9.29 Miso soup with tofu

Vitamins, minerals and secondary plant active ingredients, invigorating, detoxifying, strengthens immune system, promotes digestion, forcing spleen, containing enzymes, reduces flatulence, alginic acid detoxifies the bowel, dissolves stagnation.
Cooking time approx. 5 min
Calories p. portion: 51
3 portions
Allergens: E

Quantity of ingredients
Wakame 1 piece / 5g. (yes)
Miso 3-4 table spoons / 30g. (yes)
Soy Tofu 1/8 lbs - 2oz / 50g. (yes)
Water 2 cup / 500g. (yes)
Soy sauce 1 dash / 3g. (yes)
Onion (spring onion) 1/2 teaspoon / 6g. (yes)

Cooking instructions:
Boil soybean seedlings, wakame algae and diced tofu for 5 minutes.
Put the miso paste in the soup plate and
slowly pour over the soup. Season with Tamari sauce. Sprinkle with cutted spring onion.

9.30 Oat Congee

Strengthens immune system.
Cooking time approx. 2-4 hours
Calories p. portion: 162
3 portions
Allergens: A

Quantity of ingredients
Oat 1 cup / 125g. (yes)
Water 6 cups / 700g. (yes)

Cooking instructions:
Cook oats and water in a ratio of about 1: 6. The amount of water determines the thickness of the mash (pure matter of taste). The oats swell, so do not take much. Put the oats in a saucepan with good insulation and a heavy lid. It is important to simmer the oats after a short boil on the slightest flame, otherwise it burns. Cook the oat for 2-4 hours. The longer it cooks, the more he strengthens.

9.31 Oat flakes with aromatic spices

Stops diarrhea, promotes digestion, appetizing, harmonizes the stomach, relieves diarrhea, strengthens immune system, detoxifying and stimulating the immune system.
Cooking time approx. 25 min
Calories p. portion: 280
3 portions
Allergens: AH

Quantity of ingredients
Oat flakes (whole grain) 1 cup / 125g. (yes)
Walnuts 1 table spoon / 15g. (recommended)
Hazelnuts 1 table spoon / 15g. (yes)
Water 1 1/2 cups / 240g. (yes)
Wakame 1 inch / 2g. (yes)
Apple (sweet) 1 piece / 220g. (recommended)
Cardamom 3-4 capsules / 2g. (yes)
Lemon Balm (fresh) 3-4 leaves / 3g. (yes)
Acerola fruit nectar or powder 1 teaspoon / 2g. (yes)

Cooking instructions:
Roast oatmeal and nuts. Add hot water. Add cardamom, wakame and cook for 20 min. Add grated apple, acerola and lemon herb.

9.32 Oyster mushrooms with asparagus

Forces, reduces inflammation, improves digestion, lowers cholesterol, strengthens kidney, stimulates liver function, improves blood circulation, improves medication effect, increases appetite.
Cooking time approx. 30 min
Calories p. portion: 316
4 portions
Allergens: GH

Quantity of ingredients
Onion white 1 piece / 50g. (yes)
Butter organic 2 table spoons / 40g. (yes)
Oyster mushroom 3/4 lbs / 300g. (yes)
Sake 2 table spoons / 40g. (yes)
Parsley 2 table spoons / 40g. (yes)
Walnuts 2 table spoons / 60g. (recommended)
Asparagus (green or white) 1,1 lbs / 500g. (yes)
Salt 1 pinch / 1g. (little)
Sugar white 1 pinch / 0,1g. (recommended)
Potato 1 lbs / 500g. (yes)
Salt (herbal) 1 pinch / 1g. (little)

Cooking instructions:
Cook organically grown potatoes with the skin, otherwise prepare
peeled boiled potatoes. Boil the asparagus in salted water with a pinch
of sugar and salt. (You can cook an old roll that absorbs the bittering
substances.)
Slightly sauté the chopped onions in a pan in the butter before frying the
oyster mushrooms cut into the same pan.
Stew 15 minutes, stirring several times. Add the sake, walnuts and
parsley and simmer on low heat while you drain the potatoes and
asparagus. Finally, sprinkle some herbal salt over it.
If no fresh asparagus is available, asparagus can be used in jars.

9.33 Plum Cake

Cancer preventive effect, dehydrates the body, stimulates digestion and
binds fats in the intestine, good to fight loss of appetite, flatulence,
inflammatory bowel disease, obesity, gout, stomach ulcers, stomach
cramps, rheumatism, heartburn. Relieves pain, detoxifying, bactericide.
Cooking time approx. 1 hour
Calories p. portion: 502
6 portions
Allergens: AG

Quantity of ingredients
Curd cheese 20% 5/8 oz / 200g. (yes)
Wheat flour 7/8 lbs / 400g. (yes)
Cow's milk (whole milk 3.5% fat) 6 table spoons / 70g. (recommended)
Rapeseed oil 6 table spoons / 70g. (yes)
Honey 8 table spoons / 100g. (recommended)
Baking powder 1 package / 3g. (yes)

Salt 1 pinch / 1g. (little)
Cinnamon ground 1 teaspoon / 3g. (yes)
Plums 2,2 lbs / 1000g. (yes)

Cooking instructions:
Mix the flour, curd cheese, milk, oil, honey, salt and baking powder into a smooth dough. Keep the dough cool for 15 minutes to cool.
Lay out baking paper on a baking sheet and press the dough out to a bottom.
Now spread the plums evenly.
Sprinkle the cake with the cinnamon and bake for about 40 minutes at 190 ° C/374 °F.

9.34 Porridge

Strengthens immune system. Little laxative.
Cooking time approx. 15 min
Calories p. portion: 208
2 portions
Allergens: AG

Quantity of ingredients
Oat flakes (whole grain) 8 table spoons / 60g. (yes)
Water 1/2 cup / 125g. (yes)
Cow's milk (whole milk 3.5% fat) 1/2 cup / 125g. (recommended)
Salt 1 pinch / 0,3g. (little)
Cream, sweet 30% 2 table spoons / 20g. (recommended)
Sugar cane sugar 1 table spoon / 8g. (recommended)

Cooking instructions:
Heat water and milk and a pinch of salt till it boils. Sprinkle in 4 tablespoons of coarse rolled oats and cook to a pulp, add 4 tablespoons of fine oatmeal and let it swell. Arrange in a preheated bowl and top with cream.

9.35 Porridge with cherries

Strengthens immune system. Improves blood circulation, reduces inflammation, moisturizer dry skin. Little laxative.
Cooking time approx. 10 min
Calories p. portion: 228
2 portions
Allergens: AG

Quantity of ingredients
Oat flakes (whole grain) 8 table spoons / 60g. (yes)
Water 1/2 cup / 125g. (yes)
Cow's milk (1.5% fat) 1/2 cup / 125g. (yes)
Salt 1 pinch / 0,2g. (little)
Cream, sweet 30% 2 table spoons / 20g. (recommended)
Sugar cane sugar 1 table spoon / 8g. (recommended)
Cherry 1/4 lbs - 4oz (gutted) / 100g. (yes)

Cooking instructions:
Heat water and milk and a pinch of salt till it boils. Sprinkle in 4 tablespoons of coarse rolled oats and cook to a pulp, add 4 tablespoons of fine oatmeal, allow to simmer. Arrange in a preheated bowl and top with cream. Core and add cherries.

9.36 Quick flakes with compote or jam

Relieves pain, detoxifying, bactericide. Dissolves stones. Promotes digestion, nourishes bones and tendons, warms kidneys and spleen, forcing spleen, neutralizes Flatulence, controls excessive urge to urinate, helps to fight digestive weakness.
Cooking time approx. 5 min
Calories p. portion: 189
2 portions
Allergens: H

Quantity of ingredients
Quinoa 5-7 table spoons / 50g. (yes)
Water 1 cup / 250g. (yes)
Compote (fruits of the season) 1 cup / 100g. (recommended)
Walnuts 1 table spoon (grated) / 8g. (recommended)
Olive oil 1 table spoon / 10g. (yes)
Honey 2 table spoons / 20g. (recommended)
Vanilla 1 pinch / 0,2g. (yes)
Anise (Common Fennel) 1 pinch / 0,2g. (yes)
Cardamom 1 pinch / 0,2g. (yes)

Cooking instructions:
Put the quinoa flakes in a pan and add water. Boil for 3-5 minutes, pull from the fire, add nuts and compote. Add a dash of oil. Sweeten as needed with honey, whole cane sugar or agave syrup.
Spices and aromas: vanilla, anise, fennel or coriander, cardamom, a

little chili.
Winter: apple compote, pear compote, fruit jam.
Summer: plum compote, apricot compote.

9.37 Rhubarb and apple jelly

Antioxidants, lots of vitamin C, laxative, relieves pain, detoxifying,
warms stomach and spleen, improves blood circulation.
Cooking time approx. 15 min
Calories p. portion: 180
2 portions
Allergens:

Quantity of ingredients
Rhubarb 5/8 oz / 200g. (yes)
Apple juice (natural cloudy) 1 cup / 300g. (recommended)
Corn starch 1 oz / 30g. (yes)
Honey 1/2 oz / 20g. (recommended)
Vanilla sugar natural 1 pinch / 0,5g. (yes)
Cinnamon ground 1 pinch / 0,5g. (yes)
Peppermint 2 leaves / 2g. (yes)

Cooking instructions:
Add the cornstarch to a 1/2 cup apple juice.
Simmer the rhubarb in 1 cup of water for 10 min.
Add the remaining apple juice and the cornstarch, stir, heat till it boils
again.
Sweet with honey and season with vanilla and cinnamon. Spread the
mixture on dessert bowls and garnish with mint.

9.38 Ribbon noodles with leaf spinach

Promotes digestion, improves blood circulation, forcing spleen and
intestine, improves pancreatic function, Good to fight loss of appetite,
flatulence, inflammatory bowel disease, obesity, stomach ulcers,
stomach cramps, rheumatism, heartburn, twelffinger intestinal ulcers.
Cooking time approx. 45 min
Calories p. portion: 722
2 portions
Allergens: ACG

Quantity of ingredients
Spinach 5/8 lbs - 8oz / 250g. (yes)
Salt 1 pinch / 1g. (little)
Noodles (wheat, ribbon noodles) with egg 5/8 oz / 200g. (yes)
Olive oil 1 table spoon / 15g. (yes)
Onion (spring onion) 1 piece / 20g. (yes)
Cream, sweet 30% 1/2 cup / 100g. (recommended)
Créme fraiche cheese 1/2 teaspoon / 6g. (yes)
Thyme dried 1/2 teaspoon / 2g. (yes)
Basil (fresh) 1/2 teaspoon / 2g. (yes)
Oregano dried 1/2 teaspoon / 2g. (yes)
Nutmeg 1 pinch / 0,5g. (yes)
Pepper (ground) 1 pinch / 0,5g. (yes)
Parmesan 1/2 oz / 20g. (yes)
Pine nuts 1 table spoon / 15g. (yes)
Black caraway 1 pinch / 1g. (yes)

Cooking instructions:
Put the dripping wet spinach together with a little salt for 3 minutes ina
pot, then drain in a sieve. Then finely cut.

Boil tagliatelle in plenty of salted water.

Heat the oil in a skillet and fry the spring onions rings. Add cream,
crème fraiche, thyme, basil, oregano and nutmeg. Stir in the sauce
while stirring. Add the spinach, heat briefly, season with nutmeg, salt
and pepper.
Drain pasta and mix with the spinach. Season with salt and pepper.
Portion noodles and serve with parmesan and pine nuts. Sprinkle the
black cumin over it.

9.39 Rice congee with chicken liver and buckthorn fruit

Good to fight blood circulation disorders, thrombose, risk of embolism,
high blood pressure, a headache, heart attack and stroke. Has many
vitamins and minerals, high quality amino acid profile. Regulates the
blood pressure and blood glucose level, forcing spleen.
Cooking time approx. 3 hours
Calories p. portion: 176
3 portions
Allergens: EO

Quantity of ingredients
Basic recipe for a rice soup (Congee) 5 cups / 800g. (yes)
Chicken liver 1/2 cup / 60g. (yes)
Bocksdorn fruits (Fructus Lycii, Goji, goji berry dried 1/2 cup / 60g. (yes)
Soy sauce 1 dash / 3g. (yes)

Cooking instructions:
Cook basic recipe for rice congee with the chicken liver and wolfberry
fruits; Season with soy sauce.

9.40 Rice congee with honey pear and black sesame

Promotes digestion, supports urination, good to fight blood circulation
disorders, thromboses, risk of embolism, high blood pressure, a
headache, heart attack and stroke.
Cooking time approx. 10 min - 3 hours
Calories p. portion: 158
2 portions
Allergens: N

Quantity of ingredients
Basic recipe for a rice soup (Congee) 1 1/2 cups / 240g. (yes)
Pear 2 pieces / 300g. (yes)
Sesame, black 1 teaspoon / 3g. (yes)

Cooking instructions:
Cook rice congee according to basic recipe.
Fill pot with 3 cm of water and heat till it boils. Quarter the pears (with
the skin and seeds) and simmer them covered with black sesame for 10
minutes. Mix with the rice.

9.41 Rice with parsnips

Rich in vitamins, minerals potassium and zinc. Good to fight blood
circulation disorders, thrombose, risk of embolism, high blood pressure,
a headache, heart attack and stroke, yeast infections.
Cooking time approx. 45 min
Calories p. portion: 206
3 portions
Allergens:

Quantity of ingredients
Rice variety any 1 cup / 120g. (yes)
Water 1 1/2 cups / 200g. (yes)
Salt 1 pinch / 1g. (little)
Parsnip 3-4 pieces / 450g. (yes)
Olive oil 1 table spoon / 10g. (yes)
Sage 1 teaspoon / 3g. (yes)

Cooking instructions:
Peel the parsnips and cut into slices. Fry for a short time in oil. Add the rice and fry again for a short time. Add the water and cook it at least 30 min. Sprinkle with fresh chopped sage.

9.42 Roasted millet with Celery sticks

Promotes spleen and kidney, diuretic, promoting metabolism.
Cooking time approx. 30 min
Calories p. portion: 400
2 portions
Allergens: L

Quantity of ingredients
Millet 1 cup / 120g. (yes)
Water 1 1/2 cups / 240g. (yes)
Celery sticks 2 rods / 50g. (yes)
Herbs various 1 table spoon / 10g. (yes)
Water 2 table spoons / 30g. (yes)
Salt 1 pinch / 1g. (little)
Sage 3-4 leaves / 2g. (yes)
Cress 1 teaspoon / 3g. (yes)

Cooking instructions:
Roast millet briefly, pour over water, heat till it boils and let stand for 20 min. to swell.

Cut celery into small pieces and mix with water, salt and fresh herbs and cook for 10 min. Add to the millet.
Sprinkle fresh sage or watercress over it.

9.43 Roasted nuts

Dissolves stones. Good to fight depressions. Strengths spleen and stomach.
Cooking time approx. 5 min
Calories p. portion: 973
2 portions
Allergens: H

Quantity of ingredients
Hazelnuts 1/4 lbs - 4oz / 100g. (yes)
Cashews 1/4 lbs - 4oz / 100g. (yes)
Walnuts 1/4 lbs - 4oz / 100g. (recommended)

Cooking instructions:
Roast nuts in a pan for about 5 minutes.

9.44 Rosemary Potatoes

Reduces Inflammation, improves digestion, regenerates skin, supports urination, lowers cholesterol. Rosemary stimulates digestion, strengthens lung, promotes spleen and kidney, dries out.
Cooking time approx. 30 min
Calories p. portion: 188
2 portions
Allergens:

Quantity of ingredients
Potato 6-8 pieces / 420g. (yes)
Salt (herbal) 1 pinch / 1g. (little)
Olive oil 1 table spoon / 10g. (yes)
Rosemary 1 teaspoon / 2g. (yes)

Cooking instructions:
Cut the potatoes into half´s, apply a little olive oil on the cut surface, then salt, sprinkle 2 - 3 rosemary needles on the potatoes.
Place the potatoes on the baking tray and bake them in the preheated oven for approx. 25 minutes to 190°C/374°F.

9.45 Semolina porridge with banana

Regulates gastrointestinal function, reduces inflammation, antiallergic, good to fight blood circulation disorders.
Cooking time approx. 15 min
Calories p. portion: 307
1 portions
Allergens: AG

Quantity of ingredients
Cow's milk (whole milk 3.5% fat) 3/4 cup - 6 oz / 200g. (recommended)
Spelled semolina 2 table spoons / 30g. (yes)
Butter organic 1 teaspoon / 4g. (yes)
Banana 1/2 piece / 50g. (yes)

Cooking instructions:
Heat the half of the milk in a small pot. Add the semolina and boil it shortly in the milk. Let it swell at low heat for 3 minutes with constant stirring. Remove the pot from the heat, add the remaining milk with the snow bean and place the mush in a small bowl. Add the butter and the battered banana.
For adults, a pinch of cinnamon can be spread over it.

9.46 Soup with egg yolk

Strengthens muscles, tendons and bones, reduces blood pressure, strengthens immune system.
Cooking time approx. 5 min
Calories p. portion: 173
1 portions
Allergens: CO

Quantity of ingredients
Basic recipe for a beef soup (warming) 1 cup / 250g. (yes)
Chicken yolk 1 piece / 25g. (yes)

Cooking instructions:
Warm the beef soup according to the basic recipe for a beef broth, warm it up and jell the yolk.

9.47 Spelled with fruit and nuts

Stops diarrhea, promotes digestion, appetizing, relieves fatigue, anti-inflammatory (gastrointestinal). Good to fight tumor lesions and leukemia, is antiallergic in food allergies, regulates metabolism, lowers blood glucose and cholesterol.
Cooking time approx. 1 1/2 hours
Calories p. portion: 290
3 portions
Allergens: AH

Quantity of ingredients
Spelled grain 1 cup / 120g. (yes)
Water 1 cup / 50g. (yes)
Apple (sweet) 1 piece / 220g. (recommended)
Apricot 1 piece / 200g. (recommended)
Peaches 1 piece / 120g. (yes)
Cinnamon ground 1 pinch / 1g. (yes)
Cardamom 1 pinch / 1g. (yes)
Salt 1 pinch / 1g. (little)
Strawberries 1 cup / 120g. (yes)
Almond puree 1 table spoon / 15g. (yes)
Cocoa 1 pinch / 1g. (yes)
Walnuts 1 table spoon / 10g. (recommended)

Cooking instructions:
Put spelled in hot water and cook.

Then: Give sweet chopped fruit (apples, apricots, peaches) in a little hot water, with a little cinnamon, sauté briefly; ground cardamom and / or coriander, a small pinch of salt, the boiled spelled, berries after season. Put some cocoa and roasted nuts over it.

9.48 Supplementary nutrition

Protein-rich drink with very high energy density. Optimized protein content balances nitrogen losses and promotes protein anabolism.
Cooking time approx. 5 min
Calories p. portion: 1045
1 portions
Allergens:

Quantity of ingredients
Supplementary nutrition 1 package / 250g. (recommended)

Cooking instructions:
Use only as directed by the physician or therapist.

9.49 Sweet rice with apples

Stops diarrhea, promotes digestion, appetizing, stops coughing,
supports urination, many antioxidants. Little laxative.
Cooking time approx. 25 min
Calories p. portion: 156
4 portions
Allergens: H

Quantity of ingredients
Rice sweet 1 cup / 100g. (yes)
Water 6 cups / 600g. (yes)
Apple juice (natural cloudy) 1 cup / 120g. (recommended)
Apple (sweet) 2 pieces / 300g. (recommended)
Apricot 2 pieces / 200g. (recommended)
Cinnamon ground 1 pinch / 0,3g. (yes)
Cardamom 1 pinch / 0,2g. (yes)
Ginger powder 1 knife tip / 0,3g. (yes)
Salt 1 pinch / 0,3g. (little)
Lemon 1/2 cut into pieces / 10g. (yes)
Cocoa 1 pinch / 0,5g. (yes)
Almond puree 2 table spoons / 20g. (yes)
Barley malt 1 table spoon / 10g. (yes)
Hazelnuts 2 table spoons / 20g. (yes)

Cooking instructions:
Cook sweet rice in hot water.
Then: heat apple juice in a hot pot; chopped sweet apples, apricots or
other sweet fruit (neutral or warm), cinnamon, cardamom, ginger, a
pinch of salt, grated lemon peel, a little cocoa and simmer for a few
minutes.

Stir in the boiled sweet rice, a little almond paste, some barley malt and
heat; sprinkle with roasted nuts.

9.50 Sweet-savory barley salad

Diuretic, forcing spleen, supports urination, relaxes. Astringent, antibacterial, invigorating, calming.
Cooking time approx. 25 min
Calories p. portion: 511
2 portions
Allergens: AGHO

Quantity of ingredients
Water 5/8 oz / 50g. (yes)
Barley 1/4 lbs - 4oz / 100g. (yes)
Apple (sour) 2 pieces / 300g. (recommended)
Grapes red Handful / 20g. (yes)
Dates dried 2 table spoons (gutted) / 20g. (yes)
Almond 1 table spoon / 10g. (yes)
Curry 1 pinch / 0,2g. (yes)
Salt 1 pinch / 0,5g. (little)
Lemon juice 1 piece / 20g. (yes)
Lemon peel 1/4 piece / 2g. (yes)
Cocoa 1 pinch / 0,5g. (yes)
Cream, sweet 30% 1/2 cup / 100g. (recommended)

Cooking instructions:
Boil the barley in water.
Mix cooked barley, 2 sweet chopped apples, a handful of red grapes, about 80 g of pitted dates, about 50 g of chopped almonds, some curry, a pinch of salt, juice of 1 lemon, grated lemon zest, some cocoa.
Leave for 1 hour; Lift 100 ml of whipped cream underneath.

Recommendation: in the summer as a refreshing evening meal.

9.51 Tea Black tea (Russian tea)

Black tea improves blood circulation.
Cooking time approx. 10 min
Calories p. portion: 7
1 portions
Allergens:

Quantity of ingredients
Black tea 1 table spoon / 5g. (yes)
Water 1 cup / 120g. (yes)

Cooking instructions:
For each cup you use a teaspoonful or a teabag.
Pour green tea only with 60 to 80 ° C / 140 to 176 °F hot water, otherwise it will be bitter.
If the tea has a stimulating effect, let it draw for two to three minutes. It has a calming effect for a duration of five minutes (no longer, otherwise it will be bitter!).
Another method: Pour the tea leaves with about 70 ° C / 158 °F hot water and pour the water immediately again.
Then just pour hot water again. The bitter substances disappear and the tea gets a milder aroma.

9.52 Tea from juniper berry

Promotes digestion, diuretic, dries out, good to fight loss of appetite, diarrhea, dehydrates, gastrointestinal complaints, muscle rheumatism and pyelonephritis, heartburn, germicidal, improves blood circulation.
Cooking time approx. 10 min
Calories p. portion: 10
1 portions
Allergens:

Quantity of ingredients
Juniper berry 1 teaspoon / 3g. (yes)
Water 1 cup / 125g. (yes)

Cooking instructions:
A teaspoon of dried juniper berries for a cup of tea. Start cold and bring to the boil. Let it sit for 15 minutes, then strain.
This tea is unsweetened and swallowed, slowly drunk. The amount is enough for one day.

9.53 Tea Green tea

Green tea promotes digestion, supports urination, dissolves mucus, detoxifying, stimulates nerves, reduces blood lipids, lowers cholesterol, reduces inflammation.
Cooking time approx. 10 min
Calories p. portion: 2
1 portions
Allergens:

Quantity of ingredients
Green tea 1 teaspoon / 2g. (yes)
Water 1 cup / 120g. (yes)

Cooking instructions:
For each cup you use a teaspoonful or a teabag.
Pour green tea only with 60 to 80 ° C / 140 to 176 °F hot water, otherwise it will be bitter.
If the tea has a stimulating effect, let it draw for two to three minutes. It has a calming effect for a duration of five minutes (no longer, otherwise it will be bitter!).
Another method: Pour the tea leaves with about 70 ° C / 158 °F hot water and pour the water immediately again.
Then just pour hot water again. The bitter substances disappear and the tea gets a milder aroma.

9.54 Tomato with mozzarella

Promotes digestion, helps to digest fat, supports urination, reduces blood pressure. Affects anorexia, good to fight flatulence, inflammatory bowel disease, bloating and nausea. Relaxing and reassuring.
Cooking time approx. 5 min
Calories p. portion: 436
1 portions
Allergens: AG

Quantity of ingredients
Mozzarella 1 piece / 50g. (yes)
Tomato 2 pieces / 100g. (yes)
Salt 1 pinch / 1g. (little)
Basil (fresh) 5 leaves / 6g. (yes)
Olive oil 2 table spoons / 20g. (yes)
White bread (wheat bread) 2 slices / 40g. (yes)

Cooking instructions:
Cut tomatoes and mozzarella into slices. Serve with salt, basil and olive oil. Serve with white bread.

9.55 Vanilla cream with berries

Weakness, chronic constipation of the intestine, weight loss, laxative, detoxifying, blood detoxifying. Strengthens the defense. Good to fight fungi infections.
Cooking time approx. 15 min
Calories p. portion: 278
4 portions
Allergens: G

Quantity of ingredients
Curd cheese 20% 7/8 lbs / 400g. (yes)
Yogurt (natural, 1.5% fat) 3/8 lbs - 6oz / 150g. (yes)
Sugar brown 2 teaspoons / 8g. (recommended)
Acerola fruit nectar or powder 1 teaspoon / 2g. (yes)
Vanilla sugar natural 3 package / 3g. (yes)
Cream (30% fat) 1/4 lbs - 4oz / 125g. (recommended)
Strawberries 1/4 lbs - 4oz / 100g. (yes)
Raspberry 1/4 lbs - 4oz / 100g. (yes)
Blackberry´s 1/4 lbs - 4oz / 100g. (yes)
Blueberry 1/4 lbs - 4oz / 100g. (yes)

Cooking instructions:
Mix the curd cheese, yoghurt, sugar, acerola and vanilla sugar with a hand mixer or whisk until smooth. Beat the whipped cream very stiff, mix it under the cream. Arrange vanilla cream in portions with the berries.

9.56 Vanilla pudding

Helps to fight constipation.
Cooking time approx. 10 min
Calories p. portion: 254
2 portions
Allergens: G

Quantity of ingredients
Cow's milk (whole milk 3.5% fat) 2 cups / 500g. (recommended)
Pudding powder vanilla 1 package / 37g. (yes)
Sugar white 1 table spoon / 12g. (recommended)

Cooking instructions:
Give 3-5 tablespoons of milk into a cup, bring the rest in a pot to boil. Pour the powdered pudding into the cup and stir until free of lumpy. As soon as the milk boils, add the mixture and simmer under low heat for about 3 minutes.
Divide into prepared bowls.

9.57 Whole milk cereal mash

Reduces Inflammation, antiallergic, has a stabilizing effect on the blood circulation, lowers blood glucose and cholesterol.
Cooking time approx. 20 min
Calories p. portion: 205
1 portions
Allergens: AG

Quantity of ingredients
Cow's milk (whole milk 3.5% fat) 3/4 cup - 6 oz / 200g. (recommended)
Water 1/4 cup / 50g. (yes)
Spelled flakes 1/2 oz / 20g. (yes)
Fruit mix juice 1/2 oz / 20g. (recommended)

Cooking instructions:
Boil the milk with the wholegrain flakes and let it swell. Add the pureed fruit.

Switch between wheat, oats and wholemeal spelled flakes, as well as the fruits. So you get a variety of flavors.

9.58 Yogurt with honey and nuts

Relieves pain, detoxifying, promotes wound healing. Good to fight acute or chronic constipation of the intestine. Dissolves stones.
Cooking time approx. 5 min
Calories p. portion: 258
1 portions
Allergens: GH

Quantity of ingredients
Yogurt (natural, 3.5% fat) 1/4 lbs - 4oz / 125g. (yes)
Honey 2 table spoons / 30g. (recommended)
Walnuts 1 table spoon / 12g. (recommended)

Cooking instructions:
Mix yoghurt with honey and finely chopped nuts.

10 Effects of food

10.1 Use ingredients: recommendable

Acai powder
Aloe juice
Apple (sour)
Apple (sweet)
Apple juice (natural cloudy)
Apple puree
Apricot
Apricots juice
Berry juice
Bitter Herb liqueur
Bitter Lemon
Blueberry juice
Cherry compote
Cherry juice
Clarified butter
Clementines
Compote (fruits of the season)
Cow's milk (whole milk 3.5% fat)
Cream (30% fat)
Cream 10% coffee cream
Cream sour 30%
Cream, sweet 30%
Fox nut, gorgon nut, makhana
Fructose (glucose)

Fruit mix juice
Grape juice red
Grape juice white
Hibiscus
Honey
Kudzu
Lily bulbs
Mango juice
Maple syrup
Mascarpone cheese
Orange juice
Pear juice
Sour cream 15% fat
Sour milk
Sugar - icing sugar
Sugar brown
Sugar candy white
Sugar cane sugar
Sugar molasses
Sugar palm sugar
Sugar white
Supplementary nutrition
Walnuts
Walnuts roasted

10.2 Use ingredients: yes

Acerola fruit nectar or powder
Adzuki beans
Agar agar (kelp)
Agave nectar
Agrimony
Almond
Almond marzipan
Almond milk
Almond puree
Amaranth
Amaranth Pops
Anchovy / Sardine
Angelica root
Anise (Common Fennel)
Apricot dried
Apricot jam
Apricot nectar
Apricots

Arrowroot
Artichoke
Asparagus (green or white)
Aubergine
Avocado
Baking powder
Balm
Bamboo shoots
Banana
Banana (cooking banana)
Banchatee (green tea)
barberry
Barley
Barley flour
Barley grass powder
Barley grouts
Barley malt
Barley not peeled

Basic recipe for a beef soup
Basic recipe for a beef soup (warming)
Basic recipe for a chicken soup (warming)
Basic recipe for a duck soup
Basic recipe for a fish soup
Basic recipe for a rice soup (Congee)
Basic recipe for a vegetable soup (nutritious)
Basil
Basil (fresh)
Batavia
Bay leaf
Bean oil
Beans (green, fresh)
Bearberry leaf
Beef bone marrow
Beef fillet
Beef heart
Beef heart (calf)
Beef kidney
Beef liver
Beef lungs (calf)
Beef meat
Beef meat (calf)
Beef meatbones
Beef Oxtail pieces
Beef soup meat
Beef stomach
Beer (alcohol-free)
Beer (alcohol-reduced)
Berries of the season
Bitter orange peel
Black beans
Black caraway
Black fungus mushroom
Black tea
Blackberry dried (unripe fruit)
Blackberry jam
Blackberry leaves
Blackberry´s
Black-eyed peas
Blackthorn (Sloe)
Blue mallow tee
Blueberry
Blueberry dried
Blueberry jam
Bocksdorn fruits (Fructus Lycii, Goji, goji berry dried
Boletus mushroom
Borage
Borage oil
Boxhorn clover seeds
Brazil nuts

Bread roll
Bread with carob kernel flour
Breadcrumbs (wheat bread, bread roll)
Brie cheese
Broad beans (thick beans)
Broccoli
Brussels sprouts
Buckbean
Buckwheat
Buckwheat (roasted) Kasha
Buckwheat whole grain
Bulgur (cereals)
Burdock root tea
Bush beans
Butter (half fat)
Butter beans white
Butter organic
Buttermilk
Calamari
Camembert
Cantaloupe
Capers in olive oil
Carambola (Star fruit)
Cardamom
Carob flour, St. john's bread
Carp
Carrot
Carrot (Early Carrot)
Carrot juice without sugar
Cashews
Cauliflower
Caviar
Celery root
Celery sticks
Cereal coffee
Chamomile
Chamomile tea
Champignon
Channa-Dal
Chanterelle
Chard
Chenpi (chinese tangerine bowl)
Cherry
Cherry (sour)
Chervil
Chervil dried
Chestnut puree
Chestnuts
Chicken Blood
Chicken egg
Chicken egg white
Chicken heart
Chicken liver
Chicken meat

Chicken stomach
Chicken yolk
Chickpeas
Chickweed
Chicory
Chili (pod or ground)
Chinese cabbage
Chinese pearl barley
Chives
Chlorella (fresh water)
Chocolate
Chocolate (Diabetic)
Chrysanthemum blossom tea
Cinnamon ground
Cinnamon sticks
Clementine
Clove
Cocoa
Coconut fat
Coconut flakes
Coconut grated
Coconut meat
Coconut milk
Cod
Codfish
Coffee
Coix (seeds) YiYi Ren
Cola drink
Cooking oil
Coriander
Coriander (fresh)
Corn
Corn (fast polenta)
Corn (roasted)
Corn flour
Corn germ oil
Corn Grease (Polenta)
Corn silk tea
Corn starch
Cottage cheese
Couscous
Cow's milk (1.5% fat)
Crab
Cranberries
Cranberry
Cranberry
Cranberry jam
Cranberry juice
Cream sour 10%
Cream sour 20%
Creamer
Créme fraiche cheese
Cress
Crispbread

Crucian
Cucumber
Cucumber (bitter)
Cucumber (spicy cucumber)
Cumin (Caraway seed)
Curcuma
Curd cheese 20%
Curd cheese 40%
Currant (black)
Currant (red)
Currant (white)
Currant jam (black)
Currant jam (red)
Currant juice (black)
Currants (black)
Currants (red)
Curry
Curry paste red
Daisy
Dandelion (young plants)
Dandelion juice
Dandelionroots tea
Dashi
Dates dried
Dates red
Deer meat
Deer meat
Deer's Bones
Deer's kidneys
Dill
Duck (heart)
Duck (slaughtered)
Ducks egg
Dulse (seaweed)
Dyer's broom herb
Edam cheese
Eel
Elderberries
Elderberry blossom tee
Emmental cheese
Endive salad
Evening primrose oil
Fennel
Fennel seeds ground
Fennel tea
Fenugreek (Trigonella foenum-graecum)
Feta cheese
Feta cheese
Fig
Fig dried
Fish innards
Fish pieces mixed (fresh water)
Fish remains

Fish sauce
Flounder
Flower pollen
French beans
Fresh cheese
Fresh cheese from soya
Fresh cheese with herbs
Freshwater crab
Freshwater fish
Fruit tea
Gail plum
Galangal
Garam Masala powder
Garlic
Gelatin white
Gelee Royal
Gentian root
Gentian root tea
Ginger fresh
Ginger oil
Ginger powder
Ginkgo fruit
Ginseng
Ginseng root
Goat
Goat and sheep's blood
Goat and sheep's brain
Goat and sheep's liver
Goat and sheep's milk
Goat and sheep's stomach
Goat cheese
Goose
Goose blood
Goose egg
Goose fat
Goose parts
Gooseberry
Gorgonzola
Gouda cheese
Gourd
Grapefruit (Pomelo)
Grapefruit dried peel
Grapefruit juice
Grapes red
Grapes white
Grapeseed oil
Grass carp
Green spelt
Green tea
Greengage
Ground
Ground caraway
Guava
Halibut (Flatfish)

Hawthorn
Hazelnuts
Herbal tea mix
Herbs bitter
Herbs of Provence
Herbs various
Herbs wild
Herring
Hibiscus tea
Hijiki
Hokkaido pumpkin
Hop
Horehound leaves
Horse meat
Hyssop
Iceberg lettuce
Jasmine blossoms tee
Jellyfish
Juniper berry
Kaki plum
Kalmus
Kefir
Kidney beans (red)
King Solomon's-seal
Kiwi
Kohlrabi
Kombu seaweed (Saccharina japonica)
Kukicha tea
Kumquats
Ladyfingers
Lamb bones
Lamb kidneys
Lamb liver
Lamb meat
Lamb shoulder
Lamb's lettuce
Lamb's lettuce
Lavender blossoms
Leaf salads (bitter)
Leek
Lemon
Lemon Balm (dried)
Lemon Balm (fresh)
Lemon juice
Lemon peel
Lemongrass
Lentils
Lentils black
Lentils red
Lentils yellow
Lettuce
Licorice root tea
Lima beans
Lime

Lime blossom tea
Linseed
Linseed (crushed)
Linseed oil
Liver smoothing tea
Lobster
Longane
Loquate / Japanese medlar
Lotus roots
Lotus seeds
Lovage
Lovage seeds
Luo Han Guo fruit
Lychee
Lychee in Preserved
Lye roll
Mackerel
Mallow (Malva sylvestris) blossom tea
Malt
Mango
Manioc flour
Mare's milk
Margarine
Margarine (diet)
Marjoram
Mayonnaise 50%
Mayonnaise 80%
Mediterranean fish (cod, plaice, haddock, sea eel, mackerel)
Medlar
Millet
Millet flakes
Mineral water
Mirabelle plum
Miso
Miso black (fermented)
Miso paste (soy bean paste)
Mixed Pickles
Mold cheese
Morel (black, dried)
Morel, dried
Mozzarella
Mu Erh Mushroom
Muesli
Mulberry fruit
Mulled Wine Spice
Mullet
Multi-grain bread (gray bread)
Mung bean
Mung bean sprouting
Mussels
Mustard
Mustard Dijon
Mustard medium hot

Mustard seeds
Mustard sweet
Mutton
Mutton
Nasturtium (nose-twister or nose-tweaker)
Nectarine
Nettles
Noodles (wheat) with egg
Noodles (wheat, lasagne) with egg
Noodles (wheat, ribbon noodles) with egg
Noodles (wheat, spaghetti) with egg
Noodles (whole grain) with egg
Nori, purple seaweed, red algae
Nutmeg
Oat
Oat flakes (whole grain)
Oat flakes roasted
Oat flour
Oat fusion (baby food)
Oat meal
Oat milk
Octopus
Octopus
Okra
Olive oil
Olives
Olives green
Onion (shallot)
Onion (spring onion)
Onion read
Onion white
Orange
Orange blossom
Orange dried peel
Orange grated peel
Orange jam
Orange peel
Oregano dried
Oregano fresh
Oyster mushroom
Oyster shell powder
Oysters
Palm oil
Papaya
Parmesan
Parsley
Parsley root
Parsnip
Passion blossoms tea
Passion fruit
Peaches
Peaches (canned)

Peanut (roasted)
Peanut butter
Peanut oil
Peanuts
Pear
Pearl barley
Pearl barley
Peas
Peas, green
Pepper (ground)
Pepper Cayenne
Pepper powder (hot)
Pepper white (ground)
Peppercorns
Peppermint
Peppermint tea
Pepperoni
Pepperoni, red, pitted, halved
Pepperoni, yellow, pitted, halved
Peppers
Peppers (rose peppers)
Peppers (sweet)
Peppers powder
Perch
Pheasant
Pickle
Pig blood
Pigeon
Pigeon egg
Pimento
Pine nuts
Pineapple
Pineapple juice without sugar
Pinto beans speckled
Pistachios
Plaice
Plum
Plum dried
Plums
Pomegranate
Poppy
Pork Bacon
Pork brain
Pork fat (lard)
Pork ham
Pork ham cooked
Pork ham smoked
Pork heart
Pork kidneys
Pork knuckle
Pork Lard
Pork liver
Pork lung
Pork marrow bones

Pork meat
Pork sausage (Bratwurst)
Pork skin
Pork stomach
Pork/beef sausage (smoked)
Pork's intestine
Potato
Potato (mealy)
Potato flour
Prickly pear
Processed cheese 12%
processed cheese 30%
Psyllium seed
Pudding powder vanilla
Puff pastry
Pumpernickel (dark bread)
Pumpkin
Pumpkin seed oil
Pumpkin seeds
Quail
Quail egg
Quince
Quinoa
Rabbit
Rabbit (wild)
Rabbit liver
Rabbit meat
Radicchio
Radish
Radish (white, green, purple-red)
Radish black
Radish horseradish
Radish leaves
Raisins
Rapeseed oil
Raspberry
Raspberry dried (immature)
Raspberry jam
Raspberry leaf tea
Red beet
Red berry (without sugar)
Red cabbage
Red wine
Reishi mushroom
Rhubarb
Ribworttea
Rice (fragrance)
Rice (Gaoliang / Sorghum)
Rice (whole grain)
Rice Basmati
Rice black
Rice flour
Rice long grain rice
Rice malt

Rice mash
Rice noodles
Rice red
Rice round grain
Rice starch
Rice sticky
Rice sweet
Rice variety any
Rice wild (nature rice)
Romaine lettuce / lettuce salad
Rose blossom tea
Rose hip
Rose hip tea
Rose leaf tea
Rosefish
Rosemary
Rucola
Rusk
Rye
Rye flour
Rye wholemeal bread
Safflower (Dyer's thistle / Hong Hua)
Saffron
Sage
Sago (cereals)
Sake
Salmon
Salsify
Sauerkraut (cutted cabbage fermented)
Savory
Savoy cabbage / kale
Sea buckthorn
Sea cucumber
Seacrab
Sesame oil
Sesame oil roasted
Sesame paste (Tahini)
Sesame, black
Sesame, white
Shark
Sheep's milk
Sheep's milk yoghurt
Shiitake, dried
Shrimp
Shrimps
Skim milk powder
Slug
Sorrel
Sour cherries
Sour milk cheese 20%
Sourdough
Soy flour
Soy noodles
Soy sauce

Soy Tofu
Soy Tofu smoked
Soya Cuisine (soy cream)
Soybean milk
Soybean oil
Soybeans
Soybeans, black
Soybeans, blacks, fermented
Soybeans, yellow
Spelled (Dark) bread
Spelled flakes
Spelled grain
Spelled semolina
Spelled wholemeal flour
Spinach
Spiny lobsters
Spurdog (spiny dogfish, Schillerlocken)
St. Benedict's thistle, blessed thistle,
holy thistle, spotted thistle
Star anise
Stevia (candyleaf, sweetleaf)
Strawberries
Strawberry jam
Strawberry Juice
Sugar fructose - fruit sugar
Sugar glucose - grapes sugar
Sugar Milk Sugar
Sugar substitute (sweetener)
Sunflower oil
Sunflower seeds
Sweet potato
Tabasco
Tangerine
Tarragon (Estragon)
Tea mixture uric acid lowering
Thistle oil
Thyme
Thyme dried
Toast bread (whole grain)
Tomato
Tomato dried
Tomato juice
Tomato paste
Tomato puree
Tonic Water
Topinambur
Trout
Trout (smoked)
Truffle
Tsampa (roasted barley flour)
Tuna
Turkey breast meat
Turkey ham
Turmeric (yellow root)

Turnip
Turnips
Umeboshi paste
Umeboshi plums (Japanese apricots)
Valerian
Vanilla
Vanilla pod
Vanilla powder
Vanilla sugar natural
Vegetable juice
Vinegar (Apple vinegar)
Vinegar (Red wine vinegar)
Vinegar Aceto Balsamico
Vinegar Aceto Balsamico white
Wakame
Walnut oil
Water
Water hot
Watermelon
Wax gourd
Wheat
Wheat bran
Wheat bulgur
Wheat flakes
Wheat flatbread/pita bread
Wheat flour
Wheat flour whole grain
Wheat germ oil
Wheat semolina
Wheat semolina for children
Wheat/Rye/Gray-black bread with yeast

Wheatgrass juice
Wheatgrass powder
Whey
White beans
White bread (baguette)
White bread (pretzel sticks)
White bread (roll)
White bread (wheat bread)
White breadcrumbs
White cabbage
White dumpling bread (wheat bread cut into chunks)
Whitefish
Whole grain bread
Wholemeal flour
Wild boar meat
Wild garlic (garlic spinach)
Wild herbs
Wild strawberries
Wormwood herb
Yam root, yam root tuber
Yarrow
Yarrow tea
Yeast
Yew nut
Yoghurt vanilla
Yogi tea
Yogurt (natural, 1.5% fat)
Yogurt (natural, 3.5% fat)
Zucchini

10.3 Use ingredients: little

Beer (Pils)
Beer (Top-fermented German dark beer)
Bitter liqueur
Brown ale
Campari
Cola drink (low calorie)
Eel smoked
Fernet Branca (herbal bitter liqueur)
Ginseng liqueur
Honey wine (Met)
Lychee liqueur

Martini
Pineapple (from a can)
Prosecco
Rum
Salt
Salt (herbal)
Sherry (whine)
Spirit
Wheat beer
White wine
Wormwood

10.4 Do not use contra-acting foods

-

11 Herbs and their effects

11.1 Basil (fresh)

It has a beneficial effect on flatulence and nausea, relaxing and soothing. Good to fight emphysema, bronchitis, whooping cough, high blood pressure, headache, mouth odor, warts, hiccup, gout, migraine.

11.2 Coriander

The essential oils are appetizing, digestive, cramping and soothing in stomach and intestinal disorders.

11.3 Herbs various

Appetizing, lots of trace elements and vitamins

11.4 Cress

Diuretic, supports urination. Good to fight dry mouth, inner agitation, sore throat, diabetes, kidney stones, gastrointestinal complaints, lung problems, menstrual cramps or cancer.

11.5 Lavender blossoms

Calms the central nervous system, relieves anxiety, to fight sleep disturbances, loss of appetite and nervous intestinal complaints.

11.6 Lovage

Stimulates digestion, reduces pain. Extracts of the root are used to flush out urinary tract infections and prevent kidney gravel.

11.7 Oregano dried

It has an anti-digestive, calming and nerve-strengthening effect, helps to fight cramping stomach and intestinal disorders. The ingredient Carvacrol has an anti-inflammatory effect.

11.8 Parsley

Stimulates liver function, detoxifies. Forces urinating. Relieves flatulence. Digestive and menstrual stimulating, birth-accelerating, memory-enhancing, blood-purifying, skin-smoothing.

11.9 Peppermint

Relaxes, frees the lungs and the nose (inhale), regulates the cycle. Stimulates bile flow and bile production, antispasmodic in gastrointestinal disorders, antimicrobial and antiviral.

11.10 Rosemary

Promotes digestion, relieves bloating, strengthens lung, spleen and kidney. Affects the circulation and nerves. Appetizing. Baths help to fight circulatory disorders as well as with gout and rheumatism.

11.11 Sage

Good to fight yeast infections. The leaves have a digestive effect and are used in greasy foods. Antiperspirant effect. Helps to relieve coughing attacks. Dries out (TCM).

11.12 Black caraway

Detoxifying, immunoregulatory. In addition, the oil should stimulate the formation of bone marrow cells and generally protect body cells from viruses.

11.13 Thyme dried

Disinfecting. It stimulates the blood circulation, increases the appetite and helps to digest fat meat better. Strengthens lungs and spleen (TCM).

11.14 Lemon Balm (fresh)

Stimulating, antibacterial, encouraging, relaxing, antispasmodic, cooling, antipyretic, analgesic, sweat-inducing, virus-inhibiting. Good for colds, fever, flu, cough, bronchitis, asthma, loss of appetite, bloating, heartburn.

12 Basics of Nutrition

The basic principles of nutrition described herein are general recommendations. They are not aimed at a specific form of therapy. Recommendations concerning a therapy have priority.

12.1 Nutrition

Regular meals in a relaxed atmosphere. A warm breakfast is considered a good start into the day.
The main meals ought to be taken for lunch – supper in the early evening. Pay attention to feeling hungry or sated: don't eat too much nor remain hungry is the rule
Prepare the meals freshly from natural, regional products. Frozen, heat-conserved, industrially prepared or foodstuffs cooked in the microwave oven are rejected.
Choice of foodstuffs according to the season: more cooling food in summer, more warming food in winter.
Eat cooked food at least twice a day. Food and drinks ought to be lukewarm, never ice-cold or hot.
Raw vegetables, briefly cooked vegetables, freshly squeezed juices and mineral water are not recommended. Milk and dairy products are only included in the diet if they don't cause problems.
Don't use therapeutic recipes over a longer period without consulting your doctor or therapist.

Varied food
Enjoy the diversity of foodstuffs. Characteristics of a balanced nutrition are variety, suitable combination and a balanced quantity of rich and low energy foodstuffs (on one hand avoiding undersupply with essential nutrients and on the other hand to take to many undesirable substances).

A lot of Cereal Products - and Potatoes
Bread, pasta, rice, cereal flakes (best wholemeal) as well as potatoes contain almost no fat, but many vitamins, mineral nutrients, trace elements, roughage and secondary plant substances. These foodstuffs ought to be taken with low-fat side dishes.

Vegetables and Fruit – „Take Five" every day …
5 portions of vegetables and fruit a day, as fresh as possible, briefly cooked, or maybe one portion as a juice – ideal as a side dish to every meal as well as snack between meals: Thus a lot of vitamins, mineral nutrients as well as roughage and secondary plant substances

Daily milk and dairy products

Milk and Dairy Products every Day, once or twice per Week Fish; meat, sausages as well as eggs moderately. These foodstuffs contain valuable nutrients like calcium in the milk, iodine selenium and omega-3 fat acids in saltwater fish. Meat is favorable due to its high content of disposable iron and the vitamins B1, B6 and B12. Quantities of 300 – 600 g meat and sausage per week are sufficient. Prefer low-fat products, especially in meat- and dairy products.

Low-fat and fatty Foodstuffs

Fat supplies us with essential fat acids and fatty foodstuffs contain also fat-soluble vitamins. Fat is high in energy; therefore much fat in the food may cause overweight, possibly also cancer. Too many saturated fat acids may further a tendency for cardio-vascular diseases in the long term. Prefer vegetable oils and fats (e.g. rapeseed-, olive-, soya-oils and solid fats produced therefrom). Beware of invisible fat in meat- and dairy products, pastry and sweets as well as in fast-food and convenience foods. 70 – 90 g fat per day is sufficient.

Moderately Sugar and Salt

Take sugar and foods/drinks containing various kinds of sugar (e.g. glucose syrup) only occasionally. Use herbs and spices as well as a little salt creatively. Prefer salt containing iodine.

Plenty of Liquids

Water is absolutely essential. Drink 1-2 l liquids every day. Prefer water (with or without gas) and other low-calorie drinks. Alcoholic drinks should not be taken.

Tasty Dishes, carefully cooked

Cook the meals with as low temperatures and as short as possible, using little water and fat – this preserves the original taste, keeps the nutrients intact and prevents the production of harmful compounds.

Take time and enjoy the food

Take your Time and enjoy your Food
Eating consciously helps to eat right. The eye enjoys food, too. It's fun, invites to enjoy varied dishes and stimulates the feeling of satiety.

Watch your Weight and stay in Motion

A balanced diet and a lot of exercise and sport (30 – 60 min/day) are a healthy combination. The right weight furthers well-being and health. Thermals, directional effectiveness, digestive power

There are various criteria for judging the effectiveness of herbs and foodstuffs.

The use of certain herbs and ingredients is based on observations of the effects on the body which these foodstuffs, herbs and spices show after having eaten them. The medical science has developed following system: Every ingredient or herb has a directional effectiveness. Furthermore, there are herbs which have a special effect on certain organs.

The basic condition for a healthy metabolism is to obtain sufficient energy from food and that the digestive process doesn't use too much energy. An easily digestible meal makes content and sated, doesn't cause flatulence and fatigue after the meal. The perfect spices increase the healthiness of our meals. Very often, just small doses of herbs and spices will suffice. They are not used to make us sated, but to help our digestive organs to digest the food.

12.2 Recipes

The recipes list the ingredients to be used and the cooking instructions show how the dish is prepared. The list of ingredients shows the concerned quantities as well as the relevance for the therapy. If you find „less than mentioned", try to comply or find an alternative from the „list of recommended foodstuffs". Mostly it shall result just in a small change of taste when you simply avoid this ingredient.

Mild cooking methods: boiling, stewing, poaching, steaming
Strong cooking methods: barbecuing, roasting, frying, smoking
Balanced cooking methods: deep-frying, baking brick
Deep-freezing and warming in the microwave oven should be avoided (denaturalization).

12.3 Foodstuffs

Foodstuffs have an effect on body and soul like medicinal herbs, only a very much milder one. Dietary advice is mainly based on regional foodstuffs. The knowledge about the effects of each foodstuff and the knowledge, when which foodstuff shall be used, is based on the orthodox school of medicine. Use ecologic-organic products, if possible. As everything should be cooked for a long time due to a better digestability and very rarely eaten raw, the food agrees with everyone.

The classification of the foodstuffs according to their effect on the body is the basis in order to achieve a harmonious status of health.

Dietary advisors do not recommend certain foodstuffs for everyone. The individual diet is tailor-made for the individual constitution.

Buy only fresh and ripe fruit and vegetables. You ought to leave unripe fruit and vegetables and such with brown spots and wilted leaves behind in the market. In this case take deep-frozen goods (never ready-to-serve dishes!). Fruit and vegetables are deep-frozen immediately after harvesting and often contain more vitamins and minerals than the goods from the vegetable shelf. Whereas conserved or tinned goods contain very much less biological substances. Also, salt, sugar and others are mostly added to the latter. Never leave the foodstuffs in the water after washing them to avoid that many vital substances get drowned. Clean salads, fruit and vegetables immediately before serving.

Please make sure of the hygienic processing of foodstuffs. Clean your salads, fruit and vegetables carefully. When cooking with meat, prepare all ingredients first and then process the meat products. Clean the worktop and tools very carefully. Wooden surfaces ought to be treated with a mild disinfectant regularly in order to reduce germination.

Store fruit and vegetables separately, if possible. Harvested fruit and vegetables are still alive and emit e.g. ethylene gas, which makes other products ripen and age faster. Keep meat and fish in the closed packaging or store them in the fridge in closed containers.

12.4 Herbs

There are some basic rules for storing medicinal herbs. On principle, herbs must be protected from direct sunlight, humidity and heat.

Containers for the storage of herbs may be glasses, ceramic jars and even plastic containers. However, plastic is a rather unsuitable material and should only be a short-term solution. In case of glass containers, use a dark material.

Medicinal herbs cannot be kept for any long period. The shelf life of herbs is limited. However, it can be prolonged with suitable storage. The place should be dark, rather cool and absolutely dry. A wooden medicine cabinet, placed not directly next to a source of heat, would be ideal. Never buy large quantities of herbs so as not to have to throw them away. Label the container with the name of the herb and the date of harvesting or processing.

13 Other dietic-books

The following syndromes of dietetics, TCM or for a therapy supplement for cancer are available.

Dietetics

E001. Nutrition of the infant - baby food
E002. Nutrition during lactation
E003. Nutrition in old age
E004. Nutrition of children and adolescents
E005. Nutrition of athletes
E006. Light weight
E007. Pregnancy
E008. Full food

Protein and electrolyte - kidneys
E009. (hemodialysis) dialysis treatment
E010. Acute renal failure
E011. Chronic renal insufficiency
E012. Nephrotic syndrome
E013. Kidney stones (nephrolithiasis)

Gastrointestinal tract - pancreas
E014. Acute pancreatitis (inflammation of the pancreas)
E015. Chronic pancreatitis (inflammation of the pancreas)

Gastrointestinal tract - small intestine and large intestine
E016. Acute obstipation (constipation)
E017. Chronic obstipation (constipation)
E018. Colon irritabile
E019. Diverticulitis
E020. Acquired lactose intolerance (lactose malabsorption)
E021. Fructose malabsorption
E022. Glutensensitive enteropathy (celiac disease)
E023. Colectomy
E024. Short Bowel Syndrome

Gastrointestinal tract - liver, gallbladder, bile ducts
E025. Acute and chronic hepatitis (inflammation of the liver)
E026. Cholelithiasis (bile stones)
E027. fatty liver
E028. cirrhosis

Gastrointestinal tract - Stomach and duodenal intestine
E029. Acute gastritis
E030. Chronic gastritis
E031. Stomach bleeding
E032. Ulcus ventriculi and duodenal ulcer
E033. Condition after gastric surgery

Gastrointestinal tract - oral cavity and esophagus
E034. Stomatitis
E035. Esophageal carcinoma (esophageal cancer)
E036. Refluosophagitis (heartburn)

Special diseases
E037. Phenylketonuria (PKU)
E038. Rheumatic joint diseases

Metabolism
E039. Obesity (overweight)
E040. Diabetes mellitus
E041. Eating disorders (underweight)

Fat metabolism
E042. Hypercholesterolaemia (increased cholesterol level)
E043. Hepatic Encephalopathy

Heart and circulation
E044. Arteriosclerosis (arterial calcification)
E045. Heart insufficiency
E046. Hypertension
E047. Hyperuricaemia and gout

Changed nutrient requirements
E048. In case of fever
E049. For malignant diseases
E050. After burns
E051. Radiation and chemotherapy

CANCER
E100. Pancreatic cancer
E101. Bladder cancer
E102. Blood cancer (leukemia)
E103. Breast cancer
E104. Colorectal cancer
E105. Gastric cancer
E106. Kidney cancer
E107. Esophageal cancer

TCM
E200. Bladder - moisture heat in the bladder
E201. Bladder - moisture and cold in the bladder
E202. Bladder - emptiness and cold in the bladder
E203. Large intestine - external cold affects the large intestine
E204. Large intestine - moisture heat in the large intestine
E205. Large intestine - heat blocks the intestine II acute
E206. Large intestine - dryness of the colon
E207. Large intestine - Yang deficiency (cold)
E208. Heart - Blood insufficiency
E209. Heart - Blood stagnation
E210. Heart - Fire
E211. Heart - Hot mucus clogs the heart pores

E212. Heart - Cold mucus clogs the heart pores
E213. Heart - Qi deficiency
E214. Heart - Yang deficiency
E215. Heart - Yin deficiency
E216. Liver - Ascending Liver Yang
E217. Liver - Blood deficiency
E218. Liver - Blood stagnation
E219. Liver - Moisture heat in liver and gall bladder
E220. Liver - Fire
E221. Liver - Gall bladder Qi-Empty
E222. Liver - Cold in the liver meridian
E223. Liver - Qi stagnation
E224. Liver - Wind
E225. Liver - Wind with ascending liver Yang
E226. Liver - Wind with blood anemic
E227. Liver - Wind with extreme heat
E228. Lung - Qi deficiency
E229. Lung - Mucus-moisture in the lungs
E230. Lung - Mucus-heat in the lungs
E231. Lung - Mucus-cold in the lungs
E232. Lung - Dryness of the lungs
E233. Lung - Wind-heat attacks the lungs
E234. Lung - Wind-cold affects the lungs
E235. Lung - Yin deficiency
E236. Stomach - Bloodstagnation
E237. Stomach - Fire
E238. Stomach - Cold with liquid
E239. Stomach - Nutrition stagnation
E240. Stomach - Qi deficiency
E241. Stomach - Rebellious Qi
E242. Stomach - Yin Emptiness
E243. Spleen - Heat and moisture attack the spleen
E244. Spleen - Coldness and moisture affects the spleen
E245. Spleen - Qi deficiency
E246. Spleen - Qi deficiency + Declining spleen Qi
E247. Spleen - Qi deficiency + spleen does not control the blood
E248. Spleen - Yang deficiency
E249. Kidney - Heart and kidney no longer communicate
E250. Kidney - Jing deficiency
E251. Kidney - Kidneys cannot receive the Qi
E252. Kidney - Qi is not stable
E253. Kidney - Yang deficiency
E254. Kidney - Yin deficiency

For further information visit di-book.com.